babushka
cartwheel
mountie
babushka
ama
stovepipe
rough
casque
goate
kpie
pith-helmet
trilby
alpine
abrero
tam-o'-shante
er
homburg
derb
snood
pillbox
r
bonnet
cloch
nie
porkpie
fe
beret
tiara
ilby
busby
hal
yarmulke
biretta
leghorn
cossac

Published by Nan A. Talese,

an imprint of Doubleday,

a division of Bantam Doubleday Dell Publishing Group, Inc.

1540 Broadway, New York, New York 10036

Library of Congress Catalog Card Number: 93-60515

ISBN 0-385-47228-5

Printed in the United States of America

November, 1993, First Edition

The Hat Book

The Hat Book

Photographs by Rodney Smith

Design by Leslie Smolan

With essays by
Richard Bernstein, Mary D. Kierstead, Michael Malone,
Viola Salzedo-Gramm,
Susan Richards Shreve, Patricia Underwood
and Dana S. Wickware

NAN A. TALESE
Doubleday
Carbone Smolan Editions

New York London Toronto Sydney Auckland

A hat is a flag, a shield, a bit of armor, and the badge of femininity. A hat is the difference between wearing clothes and wearing a costume; it's the difference between being dressed and being dressed up; it's the difference between looking adequate and looking your best. A hat is to be stylish in, to glow under, to flirt beneath, to make all others seem jealous over, and to make all men feel masculine about. A piece of magic is a hat. — *Martha Sliter*

There

is a picture of my mother taken when she was twenty-one in a hat—she was always in hats—but this hat is small brimmed, tilted at an angle, and her face, half-shadowed by the brim, is wonderfully mysterious and romantic. I have had this picture since I was young, and now I keep it in the kitchen because so many people pass through there, and those new to me usually stop and say "What a great beauty," or "Is that a movie star?" or "I have a picture like that of my mother." ▲ I know it is not my mother, however lovely she is, that lifts this picture off from where it sits among many others. It is the secret of her hat. ▲ I used to die of pleasure when she came to elementary school to pick me up in a broad-brim straw hat in late spring, or an autumn-colored cloche, a cap with a long feather, or a small hat set close to her forehead with a black net veil. "Where is your mother going?" my friends would ask, their voices hushed with admiration.

"Someplace," I'd say, and that was how it felt. My mother always looked as if she were going someplace. She was not. She was at home with her children, or at our sports events or school plays, or at our dentist or doctor, or filling the house with flowers, or doing the bills. But she always kept stacked in her closet round boxes in which hats were sunk in beige tissue paper that smelled vaguely of perfume. The hats are in my closet now, no longer in boxes, piled up on top of one another, lots and lots of them, some as old as my childhood. When we are going out, my daughters and I fly to the closet and the hats tumble down in our arms. We each choose one for this day, a red beret, a black rolled-brim with a scarlet ribbon, a blue pillbox...we put them on and sail out into the world.—*Susan Richards Shreve*

The crucial ambiguity of the image lies in the hat. —MARGUERITE DURAS, THE LOVER

Off with your hat as the flag goes by. — HENRY CUYLER BUNNER, *THE OLD FLAG FROM AIRS FROM ARCADY*

His body is perfectly spherical,

He weareth a runcible hat. — EDWARD LEAR

Seeing

a child try on her mother's hat, suddenly spying the silhouette of a state trooper in the rearview mirror, watching a bride sweep by in her wedding veil: each of these sights evokes undeniable emotions in us all. One cannot be neutral in the presence of a hat. It sends a message. ⚊ When I think about the design of a hat, I consider what that message might be, and what is inside the head upon which the hat might sit. For it is with our minds that we manage and manipulate the world. ▲ The first element of design is how the hat will frame the wearer's face. The gaze is usually directed to the face and the eyes and the person sporting the hat has to be comfortable with the likelihood of attracting the attention of perfect strangers. I try to imagine myself as the woman who will wear a particular design and thus consider how serious or frivolous the hat should be. I know the decoration may divert the gaze away from the eye, so the hat wearer may be perceived as a bunch of red roses or a bird of paradise going by. In design there is a fine line separating a lovely adornment from one that is slightly ridiculous, but the true character of a hat is in how it is worn. Personal style and state of mind are what make a hat mysterious or alluring or demure. ✿ We are lucky today that one may choose to wear a hat or not, unlike fifty years ago when a hat was considered a necessity of good grooming. Now hat wearing has become a matter of personal style and a way of stimulating response. ✿ For instance, one of my greatest friends, recently divorced, had come to live in New York. She was in an elevator, wearing one of my hats, as it happened, when a gentleman entered the elevator and said, "You look wonderful in that hat." A conversation ensued and marriage followed. Hats create amazing possibilities.—*Patricia Underwood*

I look at myself in the
shopkeeper's glass and see
that there, beneath the
man's hat, the thin awkward
shape, the inadequacy of
childhood, has turned into
something else. —MARGUERITE DURAS, *THE LOVER*

All good hats are made out of nothing. —OSCAR WILDE, *PICTURE OF DORIAN GRAY*

When

I first put on a hat —that is a hat worthy of the name, with a broad

brim and a creased crown — and I happened to look at my shadow. I was expecting to see the glamorous silhouette of Humphrey Bogart as Sam Spade, private eye, or perhaps Harrison Ford in his Indiana Jones incarnation. My narcissistic striving in the purchase of a navy blue Borsalino was for a rakish elegance, modern and timeless at the same time. ➤ But in the image of my shadow, I didn't see Bogart or Ford. I saw Morris, my grandfather. ➤ Now, I loved Morris. He was a strong self-made man with roughly chiseled features, the kind of man who always wore what I define as a real hat, not a truncated, short-brimmed headpiece but a broad and baronial crown of felt pulled low over the eyes. Morris, however, was my grandfather, and he represented obsolescence, not at all the uncharted modernism I was striving for with my first Borsalino. So, when I saw him stretched across the sidewalk, I recognized my mistake. ➤ At the time, I was living in Paris, but I had already tried other headpiece styles in other places. In New York, I sometimes wore a short-brimmed wool hat that gave me a British working class quality. During my years in France, I not only bought my first Borsalino, but tried a basque beret for a while, finding it an elegant hat, but a bit of a cliché, as though I was imitating a man on a tourist poster. At a certain time in my life, I lived in North China, a very cold place in winter, and on the coldest days I came to wearing a black rabbit fur hat with tie-up earflaps that sat on my head like a dome. My silhouette took on a certain Mongol herdsman qual-ity, not at all unpleasing, considering the circumstances. ▲ I utimately discovered that a hat, by its very nature, can never be a bold new style. When you put on a hat you immerse yourself in a stylistic culture that existed long before you. And thus, it is necessarily a resurrection of tradition. It is the grandfather look that I have now 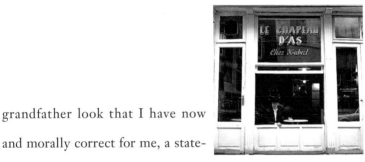 permanently adopted as culturally and morally correct for me, a state- ment of my recently accepted avuncular identity. Youthfulness as a priority has given way to the authority of the man who holds the hand of a nephew and strolls with him beneath a row of sugar maples talking about the things small boys want to talk about with the men who seem old and therefore wise to them. I am only a decade or so short of the age Morris was when he was that man to me. ✒ My latest hat is from Marshall Field in Chicago. It is black and soft and nicely indented at the crown, just a touch rakish but almost accidentally so. When I walked out of the store after buying it, a light snow was falling. I stood in front of the display window and caught my reflection mingling with the snowflakes. There, not surprisingly, was Grandpa Morris, returned from the dead yet again, and very welcome. —*Richard Bernstein*

"Look at me!

Look at me now!" said the cat.

"With a cup and a cake

On top of my hat!"　—DR. SEUSS, THE CAT IN THE HAT

Anyone

can get away without wearing a hat nowadays, with notable exceptions, such as the Queen and the Pope. They continue to be worn as a protection from the elements (cold, heat, sun), as a fashion statement (ladies-who-lunch), as decoration (Royal Ascot), as disguise (Charley's aunt). Sometimes you can have it both ways and combine the utilitarian with the decorative, such as a fur hat or a large straw beach hat. But if a choice must be made, Pretty is OK, Style is better. Such is my dark green "Genuine 100% Wool Crusher," with a two-and-a-half-inch brim and a ribbon, bought ten years ago at Ben's, in Lee, Massachusetts. In Day-Glo orange, it's worn by hunters, for obvious reasons. These hats can be found at clothing stores on the main street of almost any small town in the Northeast that hasn't yet been invaded by boutiques, and of course at L.L. Bean. They need breaking-in; when new they're stiff and unfriendly, but time softens the felt as well as the line of the brim. They thrive on abuse. Mine has been through snow, rain, sleet, and gloom of night, crushed in suitcases and pockets, thrown in the wayback of dirty station wagons, sat on by small children and large dogs. Hardship has only improved the cut of its jib. Although not born to style, my hat has acquired it. I know this because it's greatly admired by young black males, who are, in New York City at least, the arbiters of style: "Yo! That is a *bad* hat!" The brim is now wavy, the crown can be punched into any shape other than a square, the once-green ribbon has faded to an indeterminate, water-stained copper. It is a hat for all seasons, though not a hat for all occasions—it would pass muster at a wedding only on the head of a certified eccentric. It is a hat of character and distinction, and I'm planning to have it placed at the foot of my coffin when I'm lying in state at the local funeral parlor.—*Mary D. Kierstead*

Then wear the gold hat, if
that will move her:
If you can bounce high,
bounce for her too,
Till she cry "Lover, gold-
hatted, high-bouncing lover,
I must have you!" —F. SCOTT FITZGERALD, *THE GREAT GATSBY*

Some are born mad. Some remain so. — SAMUEL BECKETT

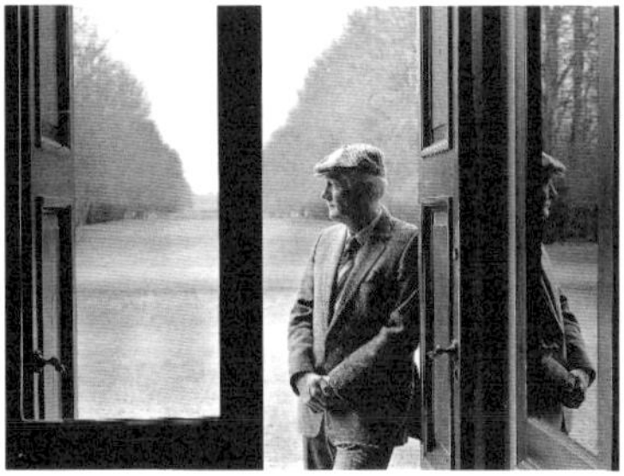

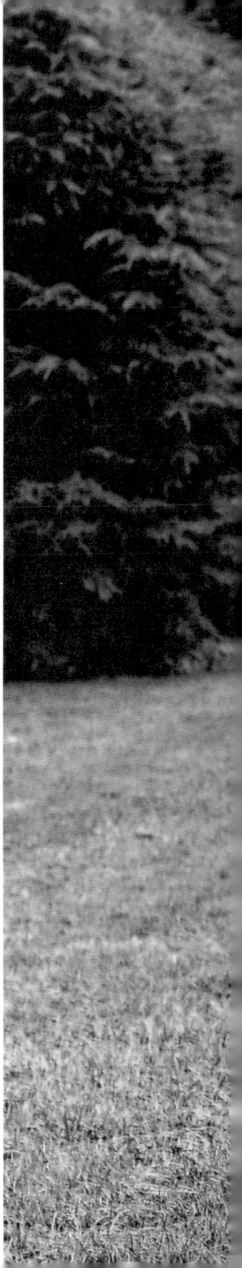

rises from the roofs of the low connected buildings set into

a hillside of the Pennsylvania Mennonite farmland. It puffs up lazily through the vents of the Bollman hat factory, maker of hats since the eighteenth century. ▪ A hat remembers the steam, and keeps hidden in its crown the secret of its strange journey during which it was transfigured from a large armful of raw wool to the distinctive shape that rests upon a head, sending a message from its wearer. ▪ It begins in a dark and sour smelling room where long sacks of sorted wool lean like tired men in a far corner, where a faint yellow light sneaks through unpainted window panes, illuminating the slowly circling dust. A furnace hums. ▪ Here, by ancient conveyor belts made of wooden slats, the wool is dipped in and out of acid baths, and let through heavy rollers that crush the dirt away. Old gears rotate, thick with grease and wool fiber. Belt chains clack unceasingly and sound

like nutshells falling on a concrete floor. ➤ Overhead in the gray-green haze hang wide tubes that cyclone the wool around the room until it is sucked up to the next floor and dropped into large bins where it rests before it is sent to be "carded." ➤ The carding room is wide, like a warehouse, and moist with steam. Everything in the room is painted that old green of New England porch furniture, and everything is worn: the machine edges, the sides of the doors, the banisters that run up and down, smoothed by the million hands that have moved across them. The engines whistle and clank. The wood floor shudders with the energy of the four huge carding machines that sit like iron elephants at the entrance. ➤ Fluff gathers along the doors, in the wheels, floats up into the light. It sticks to the end of a sneaker and is carried to another part of the room. From one of the great grumbling machines runs a long ribbon of combed wool, two feet wide and finer than laundry lint. It wraps itself around an oscillating wooden lozenge and looks like a large cocoon until it is bisected by a round blade. The two halves are lifted off by hand and weighed. ➤ Spun like cotton candy and as wide as an embrace, this cone shape rides to where the presses are. Two opposing steaming slabs close with a sigh, and all temporarily vanishes behind a veil of vapor. ➤ Felted, flattened, and half its size, the hat moves on. Coaxed by many pairs of hands, it is sent through a series of beating rubber rollers, tossed into tubs of color and vats of shellac, kneaded by steel hammers and dragged across whirring sandpaper where its sparkling felt dust spins in the sunlight. It later finds itself in a large room, vast as an airplane hangar. ➤ An army of hat-block presses, their handles angled like bayonets, stands stiffly in long rows. Around the room steam shoots up like the smoke of a hundred camp fires. A black Bolero is suspended, and the steam fingers its brim until it softens. ➤ Near the stuttering sewing machines and the  staccato chatter of the factory's million motorized parts, under the buzz of wall fans are hands that repeat the same movements again and again. This is piece work. Patient work. A ribbon is ironed and arched by hand. The welt of a brim is guided beneath a leaping needle; the careful conjuring of an effect is adroitly accomplished. ➤ From formless fluff a fedora emerges; its sinking brim and stylish silhouette held against the light. Every detail of every hat is attended by many eyes and fingers. There is simply no other way to make a hat. No better method to regard a form, and to ask: How high the crown? How deep the crease? How shall I adorn thee…with wide ribbon or narrow band? And what tilt the flange? ▲ After the mash of machinery, the magic lies in the sleight-of-hand manipulation which knows that, with each turn of a hat, the face below appears different.—*Viola Salzedo-Gramm*

Milliners never seem to have any difficulty discovering geometrical shapes wholly unknown to mathematicians. —EVAN ESAR

Hats

disappeared somewhere between my childhood and my college days. Maybe it was because John Kennedy had such gorgeous hair and therefore didn't like hats to hide it—even on that frosty day in January when he took his oath of office. He showed us there was something liberating and democratic, something emblematic of American independence in our going around bare headed. And so by the mid-sixties, hardly anyone wore hats, except in winter to keep their ears warm. ➤ But when I was growing up in the South in the forties, most grownups wore hats both indoors and out. My mother's five tall brothers lounged around the porch of the family house, all in their creamy straw Panamas with the wide striped bands; their hats as much a part of their daily apparel as their wide ties and the crisp white cotton shirtsleeves rolled above their elbows. Their wives also wore hats, not just to church but whenever they went out, even to the

store. Hats symbolized a rite of passage into "real life," where firemen and sailors, cops and cooks and priests all had the signs of their jobs clearly displayed on their heads. In fact, maybe it is because hats sit on our heads—the highest point of our bodies, the seat of our selfhood—that they have always been the most powerfully iconic article of clothing we wear. ▲ The Everyman character in the play *A Man for All Seasons* changed hats to change roles, because hats are how we say who we are, and how we find out who the other fellow is: We know a queen by a jeweled diadem, a knight by a plumed helmet, a poet by a laurel wreath. We know how to read the striped caps at Auschwitz, the crown of thorns. ▲ Hats define our relationships to others. We doff our hats to show respect. Poor Bartholomew in the Dr. Seuss tale almost lost his head because there were five-hundred hats on it, each one extravagantly flouting the respect owed the king, to whom Bartholomew was trying to bow.

To "high-hat" someone is to snub him. To throw your hat into the air, or to throw your hat into the ring, to cover your head in one place, to leave it uncovered in another—these are all distinct and significant gestures of social intercourse, lost to a hatless world. ☛ By hats, we announce our membership in a special club. You wear the black Mickey Mouse ears in front of the TV, the red tasseled Shriners fez in the parade, the pink beanie of the Leander rowing club at the Henley Royal Regatta. Your hat announces your religion (yarmulke), your nationality (Tyrolean), your job (nurse), your income (the stout plutocrat's glossy high hat that is destined to be splatted by a snowball thrown by a working-class apprentice in a cloth cap). ■ By hats we announce our status. The mortarboard says you're a college graduate, gold braid on a stiff brim says "officer"; a pointed silk miter makes you a bishop to your kneeling congregation. The peasant squeezes her black wool shawl under her chin and bows as the countess sweeps by in  her tiara. ➤ It is by mimicking the costume of rank that less lofty professions borrow authority: so the security guard has a hat like a policeman's, the hotel doorman a hat like a general's. This aping of roles by means of hats is a habit of childhood, a habit I relished. A sailor hat took me to sea on a playground raft. A paper crown made me a monarch. Wearing a policeman's hat, I stopped cars at intersections, demanding to see licenses. I slept in my faded, stained Yankees baseball cap for years, wore it all day, couldn't be parted from its magic. It made me feel a valued member of the team, a fielding friend of Lou Gehrig, batting buddy of Joe DiMaggio. ➤ It was not the hats of ordinary life that interested me, though I'd slip on a porkpie hat left by an uncle on the hall table, just to get a feel for it. No, they were hats of power and romance that I begged for. Pirate hats. Indian headdresses.

Hats of glamorous figures who had nothing to do but perfect the gestures that made them who they were. The mark of Zorro. The whip of Lash LaRue, the fastest gun in the West. I'd stand for hours in front of the mirror staring at the cowboy in a black hat with thin red ribbon on its brim staring back at me, put my hands on my double holsters, and whisper, "Draw!" ➤ By adolescence, sex had entered my hat world, and I noticed how beautiful women wore hats, not so much the flowery ones that ladies in my hometown wore to their luncheons, but the exotic ones of femme fatales in the movies. At fourteen, I started haunting the town's one "art" movie house, the Rialto, where old black-and-white movies and new exotic foreign movies were shown nightly to rather small audiences. ➤ I fell in love at the Rialto the first time Garbo stepped out of the fog from the train in *Anna Karenina*, the sable hood of her cape like a frame around her extraordinary face. Then

again when I saw the cloche on Jean Arthur, and the turban on Melina Mercouri in *Phaedra*, and the net veils clouding the secret in Dietrich's eyes, and the jaunty boy's cap hiding Jeanne Moreau's seductive hair in *Jules et Jim*. ▲ As for myself, I wanted to wear a hat like Bogie's in *Casablanca*, like Jean Paul Belmondo's in *Breathless*. I wanted the romance of Cyrano's white plume, the flair of Astaire's top hat, the jaunt of Chevalier's straw boater. ▬ Then in the eighties, to my delight, America rediscovered the romance and power and sexiness of hats. The brown hat of Indiana Jones said danger and adventure just the way Bogie's hat said danger and mystery years ago. ▪ I've long since lost that long loved Yankees cap, and the cowboy hat with the red trim. But I remember how they made me feel. Like the movies, they had that magic to tell us who we are.—*Michael Malone*

Hats divide generally into three categories: offensive hats, defensive hats, and shrapnel. —KATHERINE WHITEHORN

I'm not scared. I paid my debt to the hat. —GUS VAN SANT, DRUGSTORE COWBOY

My dear, you're the only woman in the world who'd have known the right hat to wear on an occasion such as this. —OSCAR WILDE

Here

is a sad little story <small>about class warfare. It is Saturday, November 22,</small>
1947, a subfreezing, profoundly overcast New England day; snow seems imminent. We—my father,

my stepmother, and I—are driving up the Merritt Parkway in a gleaming new Lincoln Continental

convertible, heading for New Haven to attend the Harvard-Yale football game. ➤ I love the car,

with its hundreds of pounds of tastefully sculpted chrome, its deep, polished navy blue skin, its crim-

son leather interior. As with many of his purchases, my father (a successful but chronically impecu-

nious writer) can't afford this costly bauble, and we won't have it long. Never mind: riding in that car,

especially riding with my young, sister-like stepmom, is an adventure. My newest stepmother is

twenty-four—blond, blue-eyed, shapely, and very pretty. She is the only person from the heartland

of America that my father and I have known well. Each of my father's three wives was in her early

twenties when he — now thirty-six — married them. I am fourteen. While I don't exactly lust after my stepmother, I will, a year later, be asked by the authorities at my boarding school to take down several photos of her provocatively decked out in a revealing (by the standards of the time) bathing costume. They were taken pursuant to an abortive modeling career. My cry, "but she's my mom!" will instantly resolve the matter in my favor. The three of us are a congenial group. We treat the parent-child relationship with benign irony; my father, tongue in cheek, calls me "Sonny," and I, in like fashion, call him "Father." In fact, I am the apple of his eye, and for my part, I see him as a gentle, albeit eccentric hero. ▲ Presumably, it is his affection for us that has prompted today's outing. Why else, on this frigid day, are we being dragged to see The Game? Certainly, my stepmother and I have no interest in football. ▬ In 1947, an Ivy League football match is an occasion for display. We are smartly turned out indeed: my step-mother is in her camel's hair coat and a wool town-and-country suit—a bit too chic for her long-haired, all-American good looks; I am also in a camel's hair coat, navy, crested blazer, striped tie, and gray flannels, an exemplar of youthful privilege, my father wears a blue, double-breasted Tripler suit and a dark gray, velvet-collared chesterfield. For this occasion, he also wears sporty tan pigskin gloves, a figured silk scarf and a black homburg. A small white carnation is in his lapel. How striking and attractive we are! ➤ On this day, as always, my father is an uncommonly handsome, elegant, urbane, confident figure—an Arlenesque bon vivant who hobnobs easily—charmingly—with the great and near great in literary and entertainment circles. And as always, I am proud to be with him. ➤ The game will begin at 1:30, and we arrive at the Yale Bowl with just minutes to spare.

There has been a mix-up with the tickets and, instead of being center field, twenty rows up on the Harvard side where we belong, we find ourselves high up, close to the end zone—on the Yale side. My father is irked, but in control. ▲ We do not feel simpatico with the people around us. There are no other homburgs for Harvard, prompting curious, even hostile glances from those nearby. We huddle in our places: my father and stepmother sip whiskey from a silver flask. The game is like World War I: neither side moves more than a few yards. The crowd is restless and sullen. ➤ Four minutes into the third quarter, a hard-packed snowball, thrown from above, strikes my stepmother's shoulder. Another hits me on the head, and then, in rapid succession, two more crash into my father's homburg, knocking it to the ground. We stand, turn, and encounter a sea of grinning faces: we are unable to detect the author of these outrages. We resume our seats. My father picks up the

homburg and puts it back on his head. ▪ Quickening activity on

the field momentarily diverts the crowd. Then a snowball strikes my

father on the neck. He springs to his feet and before he can turn around, a second missile lifts the

homburg from my father's head and propels it through the air. Hands are raised perhaps twenty seats

away, and to our amazement, the hat begins a journey around the stadium. Across the curved end

zone area and down the Harvard side, hands rise and fall like ripe wheat in a windy field, and we hear

little gusts of laughter. Boom! My father's homburg is out of sight and lost. My father turns and bows

deeply. The crowd, misinterpreting rage for sportsmanship, cheers. ▲ We drive back to New York

in a pall of humiliation. Harvard has lost (of course!). In a few months, the beautiful car will be gone.

In a few years, so will my father. —*Dana S. Wickware*

Why be just yourself? *I myself have twelve hats, and each one represents a different personality.* — MARGARET ATWOOD

Photography Index

Resource Guide

MEN'S HATS

BENCRAFT HATTERS
236 Broadway
Brooklyn, NY 11211
718.384.8956

BYRNIE UTZ HATS
310 Union Street
Seattle, WA 98101
206.623.0233

DEL MONICO HATTER, INC.
47 Elm Street
New Haven, CT 06510
203.787.4086

DRYSDALE'S
3220 S. Memorial
Tulsa, OK 74145
918.664.6481

FIESTA HAT SHOP
12 East Kota
Santa Barbara, CA 93101
805.965.7444

THE FOXBORO HAT SHOP
11 Bird Street
Foxboro, MA 02035
508.543.6441

THE HAT COMPANY OF SANTA CRUZ
1346 Pacific Avenue
Santa Cruz, CA 95060
408.458.9585

THE HAT GUYS CO.
1764 Broadway
Oakland, CA 94612
510.834.6868

THE HAT SHACK
317 John Ringling Blvd.
Sarasota, FL 34236
813.388.4287

HIPPODROME HATTERS
15 North Eutaw Street
Baltimore, MD 21201
410.727.4287

JJ HAT CENTER
310 Fifth Avenue
New York, NY 10001
212.239.4368

THE MAD HATTER
250 S. Limestone
Lexington, KY 40508
606.252.6209

MEYER THE HATTER
120 St. Charles Avenue
New Orleans, LA 70130
504.525.1048

MONTECRISTI CUSTOM HAT WORK
118 Galisteo Street
Santa Fe, NM 87501
505.983.9598

NADER THE HATTER
340 Worthington Street
Springfield, MA 01103
413.736.8081

NISENSON THE HATTER
25 William Street
Newark, NJ 07102
201.622.2203

PAUL STUART
Madison Avenue
at 45th Street
New York, NY 10017
212.682.0320

RAND'S CUSTOM HATTER
2205 First Avenue North
Billings, MT 59101
406.259.4886

SACRED FEATHER
417 State Street
Madison, WI 53703
608.255.2071

SHEPLERS
6201 N.W. Loop #410
San Antonio, TX 78238
210.681.8230

TOP HATTERS
855 McArthur Boulevard
San Leandro, CA 94577
510.632.5320

TOPPERS
230 Newbury Street
Boston, MA 02116
617.859.1430

TUCKER & TUCKER HATS
216 Fifth Avenue
Pittsburgh, PA 15222
412.261.2320

THE VILLAGE HAT SHOP
530 Horton Plaza
San Diego, CA 92101
619.232.4997

WESTERN HAT WORKS
868 Fifth Avenue
San Diego, CA 92101
619.234.0457

WORTH & WORTH
331 Madison Avenue
New York, NY 10017
212.867.6058

WOMEN'S HATS

ALEXANDER BROWN
9523 Santa Monica Blvd.
Beverly Hills, CA 90210
310.275.7484

AMY DOWNS
103 Stanton Street
New York, NY 10002
212.598.4189

BLAKE
2448 North Lincoln Avenue
Chicago, IL 60614
312.477.3364

CAPRICCIO
6166 North Scottsdale Road
Scottsdale, AZ 85253
602.991.1900

CHERI/CHERI KOTÉ
401 Newport Center Drive
Suite #302
Newport Beach, CA 92660
714.721.5777

COUP DE CHAPEAU
1906 Fillmore Street
San Francisco, CA 94115
415.931.7793

DAWLEY HAT SHOP
180 N. Garden
Bloomington, MN 55425
612.858.8143

DEJA-VU
10470 Lansing Street
Mendocino, CA 95460
707.937.4120

DON MARSHALL
120 East 56th St., Suite 640
New York, NY 10022
212.758.1686

DRYSDALES
3220 S. Memorial
Tulsa, OK 74145
918.664.6481

FIESTA HAT SHOP
12 East Kota
Santa Barbara, CA 93101
805.965.7444

FIFTH AVENUE HATS
7070 Aaron Aronov Road
Fairfield, AL 35064
205.785.8405

THE FOXBORO HAT SHOP
11 Bird Street
Foxboro, MA 02035
508.543.6441

FRANCES BREWSTER, INC.
301 Worth Avenue
Palm Beach, FL 33480
407.655.6700

GIMONE'S
1630 San Miguel Drive
Newport Beach, CA 92660
714.721.0111

GROVE HILL, LTD.
2010 N.W. Military Highway
San Antonio, TX 78213
210.525.8080

HARRIET'S, INC.
510 Reisterstown Road
Baltimore, MD 21208
410.484.8484

THE HAT COMPANY
OF SANTA CRUZ
1346 Pacific Avenue
Santa Cruz, CA 95060
408.458.9585

THE HAT SHACK
317 John Ringling Blvd.
Sarasota, FL 34236
813.388.4287

HATS IN THE BELFRY
1237 Wisconsin Avenue
Washington, DC 20007
202.342.2006

HATS ON POST
210 Post Street, Suite 201
San Francisco, CA 94108
415.392.3737

HEAD OVER HEELS
150 South First
San Jose, CA 95113
408.971.9606

HENRY'S
7700 E. Kellogg
Wichita, KS 67207
316.687.7200

IN BROWN'S
7353 Melrose Avenue
Los Angeles, CA 90049
213.653.7198

IT HAT TO BE YOU
Pier 17 Pavilion
South Street Seaport
New York, NY 10038
212.406.2574

LADY EMMA
454 Broadway
Saratoga Springs, NY 12866
518.587.6750

LE CHAPEAU HAT SHOP
Copley Place
100 Huntington Avenue
Boston, MA 02118
617.236.0232

LOLA MILLINERY
2 East 17th Street
New York, NY 10003
212.366.5708

THE MAD HATTER
250 S. Limestone
Lexington, KY 40508
606.252.6209

MEYER THE HATTER
120 St. Charles Avenue
New Orleans, LA 70130
504.525.1048

MONTECRISTI CUSTOM
HAT WORK
118 Galisteo Street
Santa Fe, NM 87501
505.983.9598

MR. GOODBY'S BOUTIQUE
2423A S. Shepard
Houston, TX 77019
713.523.7474

NEW ORLEANS HAT
ATTACK
620 Decatur Street
New Orleans, LA 70130
504.523.5770

NITA IDEAS, INC.
309 Millburn Avenue
Millburn, NJ 07041
201.379.7711

PARSLEY'S
HATS & GARNISHES
84 Main Street, Ark Row
Tiburon, CA 94920
415.435.6380

THE PROPER TOPPER
Union Station, West Hall
Washington, DC 20002
202.371.0639

RAND'S CUSTOM HATTER
2205 First Avenue North
Billings, MT 59101
406.259.4886

RAZOOK'S
45 East Putnam Avenue
Greenwich, CT 06830
203.661.6603

RITTMASTER
Corner of Ocean and
Monte Verde
Carmel, CA 93921
408.625.6611

RIZIK BROTHERS
1100 Connecticut Ave., NW
Washington, DC 20036
202.223.4050

SACRED FEATHER
417 State Street
Madison, WI 53703
608.255.2071

SHEPLERS
6201 N.W. Loop #410
San Antonio, TX 78238
210.681.8230

SUZANNE'S MILLINERY
700 Madison Avenue
New York, NY 10021
212.593.3232

TOP HATTERS
855 McArthur Boulevard
San Leandro, CA 94577
510.632.5320

TOPPERS
230 Newbury Street
Boston, MA 02116
617.859.1430

TRACEY TOOKER HATS
1211 Lexington Avenue
New York, NY 10028
212.472.9603

VILLAGE HATTER
1111 Newport Center Drive
Newport Beach, CA 92660
714.640.1440

VIVACE
1331 Pennsylvania Ave., NW
Washington, DC 20004
202.737.0657

WHERE'D YOU GET
THAT HAT
155 Main Street
Lake Placid, NY 12946
518.523.3101

YASO
146 Spring Street
New York, NY 10012
212.941.8506

YOUNG & ROHRIG
247 Buckhead Avenue, #104
Atlanta, GA 30305
404.814.1958

CHILDREN'S HATS

BÉBÉ THOMPSON
98 Thompson Street
New York, NY 10012
212.925.1122

FIESTA HAT SHOP
12 East Kota
Santa Barbara, CA 93101
805.965.7444

THE FOXBORO HAT SHOP
11 Bird Street
Foxboro, MA 02035
508.543.6441

THE HAT SHACK
317 John Ringling Blvd.
Sarasota, FL 34236
813.388.4287

IT HAT TO BE YOU
Pier 17 Pavilion
South Street Seaport
New York, NY 10038
212.406.2574

NEW ORLEANS HAT
ATTACK
620 Decatur Street
New Orleans, LA 70130
504.523.5770

SHOOFLY
465 Amsterdam Avenue
New York, NY 10024
212.580.4390

TOPPERS
230 Newbury Street
Boston, MA 02116
617.859.1430

INTERNATIONAL

ACCESSITY
136 Cumberland Street
Toronto, Ontario
Canada M5RIA6
416.972.1855

AU PRINTEMPS
102 Rue de Provence
75009 Paris, France
42.82.50.00

BROWN'S
23-27 South Molton Street
London W1, England
071.491.7833

FOLLI FOLLIE
19 Via Agnelli
Mantova, Italy
037.632.2575

GALERIES LAFAYETTE
40 Boulevard Haussmann
75009 Paris, France
42.82.34.56

HARRODS
87-135 Brompton Road
London SW1X 7XL, England
071.730.1234

THE HAT BOX
7 Brewers Lane
Richmond TW9, England
081.940.5362

HERALD & HEART
HATTERS
131 St. Philip Street
London SW8, England
071.627.2414

HERBERT JOHNSON
30 New Bond Street
London W1Y 9HD, England
071.408.1174

JEAN BARTHET
13 Rue Tronchet
75008, Paris, France
42.65.35.87

THE MAD HATTER
44 Clapham High Street
London SW4, England
071.720.2260

MARIE MERCIÉ
23 Rue St.- Sulpice
75006, Paris, France
43.26.45.83

MITSUKOSHI
7, Nihonbashi Muromachi,
1-chome
Chuo-Ku, Tokyo 103
03.32.41.33.11

OLIVER CHANAN
6 Rue des Rosiers
75004 Paris, France
42.77.15.87

PARIS HATS
53 Shepherds Bush Market
London W12, England
081.743.8839

PHILIPE MODEL
79 Rue des Sts.-Pères
75006 Paris, France
45.44.76.79

SCHUTZ
Am Waisenhausplatz
3011 Bern, Switzerland
041.632.0021

SUSANNE WITTRUP
10 Pfisterstrasse
D-8000 Munich 2, Germany
089.228.5903

DEPARTMENT STORES

BARNEYS NEW YORK
Nationwide

BERGDORF GOODMAN
New York

BLOOMINGDALE'S
Nationwide

CHARIVARI
New York/Tokyo

DILLARD'S
Nationwide

FELISSIMO
New York

FRED SEGAL
Santa Monica/Los Angeles

GALERIES LAFAYETTE
Paris/New York

HENRI BENDEL
Nationwide

I. MAGNIN
Nationwide

THE ICING
Nationwide

MACY'S
Nationwide

NEIMAN MARCUS
Nationwide

NORDSTROM
Nationwide

STANLEY KORSHAK
Dallas

TAKASHIMAYA
Japan/New York

DESIGNERS

ANN ALBREZIO
New York, NY
212.719.5290

CAROLINA AMATO
New York, NY
212.532.8413

ANNY-FLLE
Newark, NJ
201.623.0223

MARIE ANTOINETTE
New York, NY
201.667.3814

ELAINE ARMSTRONG
New York, NY
212.477.0481

DAVID BANASH, INC.
Boston, MA
617.482.5478

JOHN BOYD
London, England
071.589.7601

BROCARE
Los Angeles, CA
213.481.1767

JEAN-CHARLES BROSSEAU
Paris, France
42.61.51.92

GABRIELLE CADET
Paris, France
42.74.53.07

LINDA CAMPISANO
Evanston, IL
708.864.6925

CARINA
Boyton Beach, FL
407.964.9357

CAROLYN HATS
Mission Viejo, CA
714.367.1597

CHAPEAUX CARINE
New York, NY
212.777.8393

CHAPEAUX & CO.
Huntington Station, NY
516.922.4662

DEBBIE COHEN
MILLINERY
Los Angeles, CA
310.476.8031

CORRE
Paris, France
40.15.09.11

DARCY CREECH
Southport, CT
203.254.2464

CHERYL CUZCO
New York, NY
212.620.0475

DAVID
New York, NY
212.594.3170

JENNIFER DEHNER
New York, NY
212.254.6311

AMY DOWNS
New York, NY
212.598.4189

LOLA EHRLICH
New York, NY
212.366.5708

ANNA-KRISTINE FLONES
Bearsville, NY
914.679.4211

GILLES FRANÇOIS
Paris, France
43.48.45.85

FREDERICK FOX, LTD.
London, England
071.629.5706

LOUISE GREEN
Santa Monica, CA
310.393.8231

DEBORAH HARPER
New York, NY
212.227.3831

HAT ATTACK
New York, NY
212.764.0693

MELINDA HODGES
New York, NY
212.925.0699

HOODLUMS, LTD.
Waldwick, NJ
201.447.5766

ERIC JAVITS
New York, NY
212.869.7530

STEPHEN JONES
London, England
071.734.9666

KOKIN
New York, NY
212.643.8225

CHETTA KELLEY
Milton, MA
617.333.0144

HERBERT JOHNSON, LTD.
London, England
71.734.8119

CONSTANCE JOLCUVAR
Agoura Hills, CA
818.707.0960

LA SARTAN
Paris, France
42.06.11.93

J. CARLOS LEON
Palmdale, CA
805.274.4588

GABRIELLA LIGENZA
London, England
081.788.4499

MATTHEWS HATS
New York, NY
718.859.4683

MONICA MAHONEY
New York, NY
212.496.6483

DON MARSHALL
New York, NY
212.758.1686

B. MICHAEL
New York, NY
212.629.3420

JOHANNES MICHELSEN
Manchester Center, VT
802.362.3481

FRANCINE MILLO
Paris, France
45.65.26.74

PHILIPPE MODEL
Paris, France
42.96.89.02

MSM/VOGEL
New York, NY
212.989.2604

NADER THE HATTER
Springfield, MA
413.736.8081

NISENSON THE HATTER
Newark, NJ
201.622.2203

MARI O'CONNOR
MILLINERY
New York, NY
212.614.0768

FRANK OLIVE
New York, NY
212.947.6655

R. PHILLIPS
New York, NY
212.244.6067

SANDRA PHILLIPPS
Kent, England
089.275.5920

ROSEMARY PONZO
New York, NY
212.463.7971

SONDRA REDMON HATS
Santa Monica, CA
310.828.8902

DEBORAH RHODES
New York, NY
212.564.7440

ROANNE
Paris, France
48.05.05.38

BARBARA ROSS
New York, NY
212.989.2592

SAN FRANCISCO HAT
COMPANY
Berkeley, CA
510.849.2883

DAVID SHILLING HATS &
DESIGN
London, England
071.487.3179

GRAHAM SMITH
London, England
071.935.5626

TATIANNA, LTD.
Malibu, CA
310.457.3649

PHILIP TREACY, LTD.
London, England
071.259.9605

MONIKA TURTLE
Philadelphia, PA
215.232.6590

PATRICIA UNDERWOOD
New York, NY
212.268.3774

ELAINE VINCENT
New York, NY
212.768.2063

ANN VUILLE
Norwalk, CT
212.239.2256 (rep.)

WHITTALL & SHON
New York, NY
212.594.2626

MAJORIE LEE WOO
New York, NY
212.472.9792

SUSANNA WOOD
Didcott, Oxon, England
023.551.0835

HAT SUPPLY

CALIFORNIA MILLINERY
SUPPLY
721 South Spring Street
Los Angeles, CA 90014
213.622.8746

CINDERELLA FLOWER
COMPANY
60 West 38th Street
New York, NY 10018
212.840.0644

CONCORD MERCHANDISE
CORPORATION
1026 Sixth Avenue
New York, NY 10018
212.840.2720

FASHION HATS
579 Broadway
New York, NY 10012
212.226.7841

HYMEN HENDLER
& SONS, INC.
67 West 38th Street
New York, NY 10018
212.840.8393

M & J TRIMMING CO.
1008 Sixth Avenue
New York, NY 10018
212.391.9072

MANNY'S MILLINERY
SUPPLY CENTER
26 West 38th Street
New York, NY 10018
212.840.2235

SO-GOOD INC.
28 West 38th Street
New York, NY 10018
212.398.0236

TINSEL TRADING
47 West 38th Street
New York, NY 10018
212.730.1030

HAT MANUFACTURERS

ALDO HAT CORP.
48 West 37th Street
New York, NY 10018
212.629.3420

BILTMORE, INC.
139 Morris Street
Guelph, Ontario
Canada N1E5M9
519.836.2770

BOLLMAN HAT CO.
110 East Main Street
Adamstown, PA 19501
215.484.4361

CHRISTY & CO., LTD.
27 Higher Hillgate
Stockport,
Cheshire SK1 3EU
England
061.480.8731

KANGOL
Cumbria CA 23 3DJ
England
094.681.0312

LANGENBERG
HAT CO.
320 Front Street,
Box 1860
Washington, MO 63090
314.239.1860

MADCAPS
28 West 39th Street
New York, NY 10018
212.840.8540

MILANO HAT CO.
2701 Market Street
Garland, TX 75040
214.271.5559

PANAMA HAT
CO. OF THE PACIFIC
1164 Bishop Street
Suite 124 #109
Honolulu, HI 96813
808.262.2890

RESISTOL HATS
601 Marion Drive
Garland, TX 75042
214.494.0511

STETSON HAT CO.
4500 Stetson Trail
Box 1349
St. Joseph, MO 64502
816.233.8031

WORTH & WORTH
P.O. Box 539
Ridgefield, CT 06877
203.438.4934

MISCELLANEOUS

HAT LIFE
66 York Street
Jersey City, NJ 07302
201.434.8322

AMERICAN APPAREL
MANUFACTURERS
ASSOCIATION, HEADWEAR
DIVISION
2500 Wilson Boulevard
Arlington, VA 22201
703.524.1864

MILLINERY
INFORMATION BUREAU
Public relations
service to promote milliners
nationwide
212.627.8333

THE TRAVELING HAT
SALESMAN'S ASSOCIATION
OF AMERICA
c/o Annex Manufacturing
Corporation
234 16th Street
Jersey City, NJ 07310
201.659.8060

Biographies

In 1988, Leslie Smolan met a man who owned a hat company in rural Pennsylvania. She discovered upon visiting the factory that it was a magical place full of mystery and humor. Shortly afterwards, she met photographer Rodney Smith, whose powerful black and white images of workers and workplaces, and more recently fashion, captured her by their intensity, insight, and wit. When Smolan suggested that they collaborate on a book about the factory, two things happened… Smolan and Smith got married, and they both became obsessed with hats.

RODNEY SMITH is represented by the Witkin Gallery in New York, and his work has been purchased by many private collectors, corporations and museums. In 1983 his photographs of Israel were published by Houghton Mifflin in a book entitled *In the Land of Light*. Mr. Smith has recently begun to photograph men's and women's fashion for Bergdorf Goodman, Saks, Nieman Marcus, *Taxi* and *Lears* magazine.

LESLIE SMOLAN is the acclaimed designer of the *Day in the Life* book series, cookbooks for Stewart Tabori and Chang and Chronicle Books, and educational publishing programs for Houghton Mifflin, McGraw-Hill, and Macmillan. For sixteen years, Smolan and her partner Ken Carbone, have built an international reputation for design excellence. Other clients include the Louvre, the Museum of Modern Art, Tiffany & Co., Steuben, and American Express.

RICHARD BERNSTEIN is a reporter at *The New York Times*. He is the author of *From the Center of the Earth: The Search for the Truth about China*, and *Fragile Glory: A Portrait of France and the French*. He is currently finishing a book on multiculturalism and political correctness.

MARY D. KIERSTEAD is on staff with *The New Yorker* and resides in Manhattan.

MICHAEL MALONE is the critically acclaimed author of nine books, including *Time's Witness*, *Uncivil Seasons*, and *Dingley Falls*. He is currently head writer of the ABC television drama *One Life to Live*.

VIOLA SALZEDO-GRAMM is a classical painter residing in Manhattan. She also wears many hats.

SUSAN RICHARDS SHREVE is the author of nine novels, most recently *Daughters of the New World*, and *The Train Home*, just published.

PATRICIA UNDERWOOD is a reknowned hat designer living and working in New York. She has won multiple awards for her work, including the Coty Award in 1982.

DANA S. WICKWARE is a writer and journalist. He lives on the Connecticut shore.

Acknowledgements

This book would not have been possible without the generous assistance of the following individuals:

NAN A. TALESE, who from the very beginning, understood the spirit of the project, believing in the magic of photography, design and hats.

JARMON DOWNS, Heritage Press, Dallas, Texas, for his early and ongoing enthusiasm for the book, and vision on how to translate our ideas to paper.

SUE MEDLICOTT, Allethaire Press, Hadley, Massachusetts, for helping us understand the intricacies of dry trap printing, and providing critical technical information to assist us in developing the separation process for this book.

JENNIFER DOMER, Carbone Smolan Associates, for her tireless commitment to exploring the design possibilities, and creating the framework for the photographs.

SAMUEL PETTENGILL, for his darkroom skills in making exquisite black and white prints.

JAMES HALTEMAN, Heritage Press, Dallas, Texas, for his keen vision and sensitive translation of the photographs to tritone separations.

LAURA SHORE and Mohawk Paper Mills, Cohoes, New York, for producing a truly beautiful sheet of paper, and enthusiastically supporting the book to the design community.

RICK SMOLAN, for the generosity of sharing his years of experience in launching unusual book projects and finding ways to get others excited about them.

NICHOLAS CALLAWAY, for providing inspiration for exquisitely produced books, and being a sounding board for our visual and marketing ideas.

JEFF STONE, for generously helping us think through the publishing and distribution aspects of the book.

SHERYL SHADE and ELIZABETH HARRISON, for their dedicated research and marketing.

BILL STEIN, Bollman Hat Company, Adamstown, Pennsylvania, for providing the inspiration for this book, and allowing us to experience the magic of his factory and the hat making process.

Lastly, we would like to thank the following for their valued advice: Rhoda Albom, Richard Benson, Casey Bush, Elsa Cameron, Ken Carbone, Richard Currier, Don Foster, Elayne Garofolo, Kim Johnson Gross, Claire Gruppo, Rita Jacobs, Anne Janas, Peggy Roalf, Alma Mazer, Charlie Melcher, Cindy Miller, Thomas Palmer, Stefan Schinzinger, Jay Self, Aviva Slesin, Martha and Conrad Vogel

Rodney Smith and Leslie Smolan, September 1993

This book was designed
by Leslie Smolan and Jennifer Domer,
and packaged by Carbone Smolan Associates,
New York City. Photographs are by Rodney Smith,
Snedens Landing, Palisades, New York. The text was set
in Adobe Janson Text. The 300 linescreen separations were
printed dry trap by Heritage Press, Dallas, Texas, on White
Mohawk Superfine Smooth, 100 pound text produced by
Mohawk Paper Mills, Cohoes, New York. The flyleaf is
Mokuba #6. The binding is by Ellis Bindery, Dallas, Texas.
The Hat Book was first printed in an edition of twenty-five thousand copies.

tricorne

pillbox   cloche

tricorne   wimple   pa

snood   gainsb

canotier   biretta   po

cornette   leghorn

babushka   so

mitre   bow

ossack   pith-helmet

skimmer   bump

bonnet   chechia   be

derby   sombrero

owler   skullcap

marquis   mountie

tricorne   beret   pill